Legend of Damu – Part 2

R. Kalyana Krishnan

BlueRose ONE .com DIY
Stories Matter
NewDelhi • London

BLUEROSE PUBLISHERS
India | U.K.

For permissions requests or inquiries regarding this publication,
please contact:

BLUEROSE PUBLISHERS
www.BlueRoseONE.com
info@bluerosepublishers.com
+91 8882 898 898
+4407342408967

ISBN: 978-93-7139-290-7

First Edition: July 2025

BIRLA
MANDIR

PREFACE

In the first edition of *Legend of Damu*, readers were introduced to the unassuming yet unforgettable world of Damodar—a man who stumbles into chaos and somehow emerges a hero. His adventures, often born from innocent mistakes or his signature curiosity, captured hearts across the ages.

This second edition Legend of Damu Part -2, picks up where the first left off, beginning with the unforgettable moment in "The Trumpet That Tamed the Tiger" where Damu unknowingly saves a child from danger with nothing but a toy trumpet and his calm demeanour. Eight fresh episodes follow, each more engaging than the last, blending humour, warmth, suspense, and simple wisdom.

From temples to traffic, tigers to tech-smugglers, the family journeys with Damu through yet another wave of unpredictable events—often perilous, occasionally hilarious, but always rooted in his gentle, well-meaning spirit. In the final tale set in Hyderabad, Damu's accidental involvement leads to the unravelling of a smuggling ring, proving once again that heroism sometimes wears chappals and carries a lunchbox.

These stories are not just adventures—they're reminders of how one ordinary man, supported by his strong-willed wife Lakshmi and sharp-minded daughter Vidya, turns the everyday into the extraordinary.

As you read on, I hope these tales entertain you, make you smile, and most of all, remind you of the magic hidden in life's smallest moments.

CONTENTS

"The Trumpet That Tamed the Tiger"

It was the holiday season, and the air was ripe with excitement. Damu, Lakshmi, and little Vidya packed their bags for a much-awaited visit to Damu's grandfather's house in Lucknow. It was an old haveli with creaking stairs, high ceilings, and mango trees that whispered family tales to the wind.

On their second day there—an unusually sunny Saturday—Vidya bounced up to her father with twinkling eyes. "Appa, can we go to the zoo today? Please, please, please?"

Damu, momentarily roused from his daydream about Mysore Pak and missed deadlines, blinked. "Zoo? Ah, yes, animals. Good idea."

Lakshmi smiled, "We could all use a break. Let's make it a family outing."

By 10:15 AM, the trio stood at the gates of the Lucknow Zoo, tickets in hand and snack bags slung over their shoulders. As they entered, Vidya's excitement exploded. "Look, Amma! Monkeys! That one is carrying its baby—it looks so cute!

"Damu scratched his head unconsciously.

They strolled from enclosure to enclosure: elegant deer, sleepy rhinos, elephants with flapping ears, giraffes necking through branches, and birds with feathers more vivid than Holi colours. Vidya read every animal plaque aloud with the seriousness of a documentary narrator. Damu, meanwhile, wandered ahead like a philosopher lost in a jungle of thoughts, half watching the lions, half thinking about a missed LIC premium payment.

By 12:30 PM, tired and slightly hungry, they settled on a bench near the zoo's restaurant—just a stone's throw from the tiger enclosure. Vidya munched on murukku, Lakshmi sipped juice, and Damu, the ever-helpful husband, went to fetch bottled water and chips.

Now, the tiger enclosure was a grand affair carved from natural rock, with two entrances: one led to an open field with trees and a pool, the other—a maintenance gate—opened to the visitor path and was only used by zoo staff. Normally, strict rules ensured that both gates were never open at the same time. But on this fateful day, someone didn't read the zoo manual carefully enough.

A zookeeper was busy cleaning the cave. Unaware that the inner gate hadn't been shut properly, he went off to fetch the tiger's lunch. But someone else got lunch ideas first. A curious tigress, with the grace of a ballet dancer and the hunger of a Sunday faster, squeezed through the slightly open gate and sauntered out... into the public space.

Panic Ensued.

People screamed. Some ran. Some climbed trees like squirrels in jeans. A few wise ones bolted into the restaurant and slammed the doors shut. Lakshmi and Vidya, too, rushed towards the restaurant with the others, praying that Damu, who had gone to get water and chips, would find a safe place to hide. The zookeeper, standing on top of the enclosure, nearly fainted, then scrambled to secure the remaining gates.

A young mother, caught unawares, stood frozen with her three-year-old. As the crowd vanished and her eyes met the advancing tiger, she fainted in shock. Her child, clutching a plastic toy trumpet, began to cry beside her.

Enter Damu. Chips in one hand, water bottles dangling from the other, humming an old Ilaiyaraaja tune.

He spotted the child crying beside the unconscious woman. "Poor baby," he muttered, kneeling. "Must be hungry."

He took the toy trumpet from the child. "Here, Uncle will show you how it's done." And with a mighty puff, Damu blew the trumpet like a bugler in a village parade.

PPPAAARAAAMMMM!!!

The surroundings had fallen silent, and people stood frozen in fear, watching the unfolding drama. In that tense stillness, the sudden, high-pitched blast tore through the air like a surprise firecracker.

The tigress, already just inches away, screeched to a halt. Startled out of her feline poise, she blinked, let out a sharp hiss, and—without further hesitation—spun around and dashed back through the enclosure gate. The zookeeper, quick on his feet at last, slammed it shut just in time.

Damu, oblivious to the drama behind him, was now sprinkling water on the lady's face. "Amma, wake up. Don't worry, the child is not crying now. He even played the trumpet for me."

The lady stirred, opened her eyes, recollected what had happened a short while ago, and sobbed as she hugged her child. By now, the visitors from the trees had descended like parrots in reunion mode. A crowd gathered. Whispers turned into cheers. People clapped. One teen yelled, "He saved them both!" Another proudly declared, "It's already on Facebook Live, bro!"

Damu looked around, slightly embarrassed. "Eh? What did I do?"

Back at the restaurant, Lakshmi and Vidya, having watched the entire episode through the window, ran out the moment the gates were secured. Vidya flung her arms around her father. "Appa, you're a HERO!"

Lakshmi touched his arm tenderly. "You just saved lives."

Damu blinked. "I... did? I only blew a trumpet and gave water!"

Just then, Lakshmi's phone rang. It was Inspector Ranjith from Kedarpur. "Saw the video! Lakshmi. Only Damu could face a tiger like that without even knowing it. Hats off!"

The Zoo director soon arrived with his staff. He shook Damu's hand vigorously, "Sir, you've just prevented a major tragedy. I'd like to thank you on behalf of the entire city."

"Err... thank you, sir. I... um... just bought chips," Damu mumbled.

By evening, news channels ran the footage with headlines like **"Toy Trumpet Saves the Day!"** and **"Fearless Hero Outwits Tiger"**. Back home, Vidya was already rehearsing how she'd narrate the story at school. Lakshmi couldn't stop smiling. Damu's in-laws, hearing of the news, welcomed him back like a returning war hero. Someone even played nadaswaram music on their phone for dramatic effect.

And Damu? He simply said, "Next time, we'll visit the Aquarium. It will be much safer."

The Day Damu Blocked a Disaster

Kedarpur was a town of surprises. Sometimes those surprises came in the form of pop-up vegetable stalls in the middle of the road, and sometimes, in rare cases, they came from the sky like on this day. It was the second week of June, and the morning had started like any other. Birds chirped, shopkeepers swept the front of their stores, and Damu, our ever-dependable man-of-the-moment, had promised Lakshmi he'd get fresh vegetables. A harmless errand… or so he thought.

By noon, the sky changed its mind. The bright sun pulled its curtains shut, and Kedarpur was draped in a thick blanket of ominous grey. At 12:30 pm, the weather observatory confirmed what everyone's knees and creaky windows were already suspecting: *a heavy downpour was on the way*. The district collector didn't waste time. All schools and colleges were ordered to shut immediately and send students home.

Though the drizzle became intense, Damu remained blissfully unaware. He was busy selecting the ripest tomatoes and bargaining with a vendor over the price of coriander. The rain hit with vengeance by 1:30 pm—angry, wild, and unforgiving. People began abandoning their plans, running for shelter, their umbrellas flipping inside-out in the wind like clumsy parachutes. Government workers rushed to low-lying areas, beginning evacuations as water started invading homes.

Meanwhile, Damu, now armed with a bag full of vegetables and half-soaked under his raincoat, mounted his old scooter and started for home. What was supposed to be a simple ten-minute ride turned into a battle through wind, water, and wildly swaying trees.

As he inched forward, he reached a culvert near the bend of a lonely road, where water had begun stagnating ominously. He noticed the flow was blocked. Thinking no further than his usual problem-solving style, Damu parked his scooter in the middle of the road—the *safest* visible patch—and waddled toward the water's edge.

He picked up a broken tree branch and began poking the debris clogging the flow, muttering to himself, "These drains are like my uncle's nose. One small block, and it all stops working."

Just then, a school bus arrived on the same road. Inside were nearly forty children, already jittery from the thunder and swaying trees. The driver, already grumpy, saw the scooter parked right in the middle of the road and lost his cool.

"Hey! Move your scooter! Are you planting it there or parking it?" he shouted through the window, leaning out, trying to spot the mysterious man in a muddy raincoat who dared to park like a monument.

Damu was too engrossed to respond. He was deep in "rescue-the-drain" mode, still jabbing at the muck. Just as the driver prepared to step out and give him a piece of his mind, a huge gust of wind roared like a lion.

CRAAACK!

Everyone froze.

A massive tree beside the culvert snapped from its roots and came crashing down, *exactly* at the spot where the scooter was parked. The thunderous fall shook the ground, water splashed like a wave in a swimming pool, the scooter toppled, and vegetables went flying in all directions. A tomato landed squarely on the bus's windshield, startling everyone inside. Children screamed. The driver's jaw dropped.

For a moment, time stopped.

Had the bus moved ahead, it would've been *under* that tree. The driver, now pale, shivered at the thought. His anger melted like ice in hot tea. Meanwhile, Damu, drenched and speckled with wet leaves, turned around and blinked, "My God?" on seeing the huge tree falling in front of his scooter.

The bus driver leapt out, his voice quivering. "Sir... you... You just saved all of us."

Damu blinked. "Saved? I was just poking the drain. And who's going to save my scooter and vegetables now?"

The driver quickly invited him onto the bus and called the school management to report what had happened. Damu, still squishing with every step, pulled out his phone and rang Ranjith, his friend and local police officer.

"Ranjith, I think something fell. A tree. Also, I may have blocked traffic. But for good reason. Also... you might want to bring a crane."

Ranjith, ever-ready for action, set off in his jeep with a few constables. When he arrived, his eyes widened at the sight of the fallen giant tree sprawled across the road.

The bus driver eagerly narrated the whole sequence—how Damu's inconvenient parking had ironically become their lifesaver. "If he had moved the scooter, we'd have been under that tree, Sir. That man—Damu—he saved all these kids."

Ranjith shook his head in awe. "Only Damu," he muttered, half-laughing, "can cause traffic, a rescue, and a miracle—all at once."

As the rains softened, help arrived. The municipal workers cleared the road with a bulldozer, lifting the giant tree while curious onlookers began to gather. The school principal, alerted by the driver, reached the spot, comforted the frightened children, and sent out messages to all parents assuring their safety.

Before the bus moved again, the principal and Ranjith joined hands to thank Damu. His muddy raincoat, tilted helmet, and slightly bewildered look only added to the moment.

"We must really consider giving you a medal, Damu," the principal said. "But first—shall we get you a new bag of vegetables?"

Damu chuckled in a lighter vein. "Yes, and maybe a new scooter too. Mine just had a head-on collision with a tomato."

The children, now recovering from their shock, erupted in giggles. One boy waved and shouted, "Uncle, you're like a superhero! But instead of a cape, you wear a raincoat!"

Damu grinned, raising a hand like a politician acknowledging a crowd. "Raincoat Man saves the day!" he announced, striking a soggy pose.

As the bus rolled away and the crowd dispersed, Ranjith gave Damu a hearty slap on the back. "Let's get you a hot cup of tea. You've saved lives... and possibly set a record for heroic drain cleaning."

Damu sighed. "Next time, I'm just ordering groceries and vegetables online."

The Paperweight of Fortune

In bustling Kedarpur, where ancient whispers tangled with modern noise, an age-old story was about to rewrite itself — thanks to one man's deep love for paperweights.

It all began in the dusty corner of ***Chippu & Cheeni Antiques***, where Damu, the ever-curious civil servant with an eye for the *affordable and useless*, spotted a peculiar-looking lump of metal.

"This will look nice on my office table," he mumbled, convinced that a ₹100 relic was a better investment than stocks — and certainly more tolerable than his boss's motivational posters pinned above the desk.

What Damu didn't realise was that he had just purchased half of a legendary artefact, dating back to a time when the mighty Maharaja of Kedarpur ruled the land and hoarded his riches like squirrels on a sugar rush.

Unbeknownst to him, the second half of the artefact lay under bright museum lights, directly beneath a board that read: ***Photography Strictly Prohibited***. It had remained there since the government took over the Maharaja's estate after the Queen's demise, turning the palace into a museum and his treasures into public exhibits — and some, accidentally, into scrap.

Damu's 12-year-old daughter, Vidya, had a sharp mind and an even sharper curiosity. One look at the artefact, and she was hooked.

She posted a reel online titled ***"My Dad's Coolest Paperweight 😎 #AncientOrNot,"*** and within hours, the video spread faster than Damu's homemade tamarind rice during office lunches.

Vidya, a history buff with instincts sharper than Sherlock's, got a hunch. Her friend Geetha, equally nerdy and dramatic, gasped and said, "Go to the Museum. Go alone. Be mysterious. It's how all great discoveries begin."

On her first visit, Vidya browsed books but missed the artefact. That night, she dreamt of spinning scripts and treasure maps. The next morning, she launched a research spree — tabs flying open on her desktop like fireworks on Diwali night.

She stumbled upon an old entry about a Maharaja's treasure rumoured to be buried near a rivulet beyond a hillock. The key to the treasure? A code split across two ancient artefacts — the very ones she believed she had found.

On her second museum visit, she dusted off a forgotten library book and found the proof — a picture titled ***"The Twin Artefacts."*** She nearly choked on her excitement. Memorising every swirl and squiggle, she dashed to the display section. There it was — the second artefact, encased in glass.

Museum rules said no photos. So she used the most powerful camera of all — her brain.

Meanwhile, in the Dark Alleys of Crime...

Across town, Rocky, a college dropout turned black-market smuggler, was sipping his morning tea when Jack, his 58-year-old adviser and retired pickpocket (whose knees creaked louder than a rusty gate), squinted at a phone.

"Wait... pause that reel," Jack said, pointing at Vidya's video.

"That thing... I saw it. In the Museum! That's not a toy — it's a fortune!"

Minutes later, Rocky and Jack entered the Museum. With a hidden mobile camera tucked in his shirt, Rocky hovered near the display like a pigeon in a jewellery store. CCTV footage later captured everything — suspicious pauses, Jack's theatrical coughs, and Rocky walking away like he'd just shoplifted a potato.

They slinked into the Museum library. Rocky "casually" asked for the same book Vidya had used. He saw her name in the register and grinned wickedly.

"So... the girl knows something."

That evening, Damu's scooter was missing. Lakshmi's tiffin box had mysteriously moved shelves. His office drawer looked disturbed.

The truth? Rocky and Jack had broken into their house. They found the ***replica*** Vidya had made for a school project and stole it — thinking it was the original.

The *real* artefact, ironically, was tucked safely in Damu's office bag, brought daily to work and placed lovingly on top of paper stacks.

Vidya, sensing trouble, confided in Inspector Ranjith — Damu's closest friend and the town's sharpest cop.

"Smart girl," Ranjith said. "But now you're in danger."

He handed her a GPS tracker shaped like a hair clip.
"Wear it. Don't remove it."

When Rocky realised they'd stolen a replica, he panicked. But with both videos — Rocky's hidden footage and Vidya's viral reel — Jack managed to decode part of the script.

Still, they needed Vidya to unlock the rest.

One foggy morning, as Vidya stepped out to meet Geetha, a van screeched to a halt.

She was kidnapped.

Fortunately, her GPS hair clip blinked like a disco light on Ranjith's tracker. Damu, Lakshmi, and Ranjith raced toward the signal, leading them to the hillock by the rivulet, just as legend had described.

Inside a cave, Rocky pointed a gun at Vidya and shouted, "Crack the code! Or else..."

Vidya, calm and composed, studied the inscriptions. "Step on the tiger-tile to open the tunnel," she read silently.

Ranjith burst in. "Police! Drop the weapon!"

Rocky grabbed Vidya. "Drop your gun, or she's gone."

Ranjith froze.

Jack chuckled. "We win!"

Just then, Damu — who had slipped on a rock in his usual clumsy style — landed hard on a particular stone.

CLUNK! A hidden passage creaked open.

Everyone stared.

Rocky's jaw dropped. Jack blinked like a startled owl. Ranjith seized the moment, lunged at Rocky, and the gun flew into the air...

...landing at Damu's feet.

Damu bent to pick it up.

"Appa, stop!" Vidya screamed. "It might be—"

Too late.

Damu instinctively pulled the trigger. Nothing happened.

Vidya grabbed it gracefully and pointed it at Jack with the poise of a Bollywood heroine.

"Don't move."

Jack raised his hands. "She means business!"

Seconds later, Ranjith's backup team stormed in and handcuffed the two criminals.

The Maharaja's treasure — gold coins, rare jewels, antique scrolls, and even a ruby-studded spoon shaped like a peacock — was handed over to the Government of India. The press called it ***"The Discovery of the Decade."***

The spotlight shone on a 12-year-old historian-in-the-making and her slightly absent-minded father.

The Museum's CCTV footage confirmed everything: Rocky and Jack's shady behaviour, Jack's noisy coughing fits, Rocky's shirt-pocket camera trick. That evidence sealed the case — and the two criminals — in court.

A week later, while checking recovered items from the hideout, Ranjith found Damu's old scooter — slightly dusty but still humming with loyalty.
Lakshmi beamed. "At least *one* thing found its way back!"

Damu had his explanation:

"I told Lakshmi these antiques attract trouble. But nooo, she said. 'Buy it, use it as a paperweight'... now see!"

Still, he was hailed as a hero — praised in newspapers, cheered by neighbours, and even admired by his boss, who finally muttered:

"Damu, even your mistakes are productive!"

Vidya was honoured at her school assembly. The Principal declared proudly:

"This is why we should read history books — not just scroll cat videos!"

As for Jack and Rocky, locked in separate cells, Jack grumbled, "Outsmarted by a girl... and a paperweight."

Rocky groaned, "And a man who opens secret tunnels by accident."

Now preserved in a high-tech glass enclosure, ***"The Twin Artefacts"*** bear a new label:

"Found by accident. Guarded with Care."

And Damu?

He still carries a paperweight to the office — only now, it's stamped:

"Replica – For Office Use Only."

Damu and the Delay That Saved Lives

After months of planning, Damu, Lakshmi, and their daughter Vidya were finally off on a long-awaited vacation to Kerala. The journey from Dehradun to Cochin by train had been a pleasant one, filled with scenic views and exciting conversations. Cochin, with its mix of colonial charm and coastal breeze, welcomed them warmly.

Upon arrival, the family made their way to the Government Tourist Office, where they were briefed about various tour packages. Wayanad, a hill station famed for its dense forests and cool climate, caught their interest immediately. It was around 90 km away, nestled high in the Western Ghats. Without hesitation, Damu booked a package tour that included a bus ride to a beautiful resort in the hills.

By 10:00 AM, they boarded the tourist bus, joining a group of enthusiastic fellow travellers. Everyone settled into their seats, eager to experience the enchanting journey through Kerala's famed landscapes. The bus passed lush paddy fields, meandering rivers, and quaint villages. Initially, the weather was mild, warm, but breezy. Laughter and chatter filled the vehicle.

But as the bus entered the winding ghat section, the sky darkened ominously. Thick clouds loomed overhead, and within minutes, sheets of rain began pouring down. The clock struck noon just as the driver slowed the vehicle at the base of the hill. Visibility was poor, and the roads ahead looked dangerously slippery.

Sensing the worsening weather, the driver pulled over near a rustic roadside *Dhaba*. After a brief discussion with his tourist guide, "Let's halt here till the rain eases," he announced. Everyone alighted, shaking off the mild discomfort from the long ride. They were soon engrossed in the comforting aromas of local Kerala cuisine and steaming cups of tea. The patter of rain on the tiled roof added to the ambience.

For the next hour, the group enjoyed their lunch and debated whether the tour would continue or be postponed. Then, around 1:30 PM, the rain slowed to a drizzle, and by 2:00 PM, sunrays broke through the thick clouds, casting a golden sheen over the wet landscape.

"Looks like the worst is over," the driver said cheerfully. The Tourist guide added, "Please be ready in 15 minutes. We'll continue uphill to the resort."

Relieved, everyone began preparing to board. As bags were loaded back into the luggage compartment, Damu leaned over to Lakshmi, "Let me just find a washroom and be back in five minutes."

He walked toward the back of the *Dhaba*, where he found a small brick-built toilet. Entering, he struggled with the rusted tower bolt. With effort, he managed to slide it shut. After relieving himself, he tugged at the bolt to open the door—but it wouldn't budge. He pulled harder. The rusted metal creaked, then snapped—the knob came off in his hand.

"Uh-oh," he muttered, trapped.

He banged on the door and shouted, "Hello? Anybody out there?" But the washroom stood at the far back, separated from the main *Dhaba* by a garden patch and the kitchen wall. No one heard him.

Meanwhile, the driver and the guide had finished headcounts and realised someone was missing. Lakshmi, puzzled, said, "He just went to the washroom. He should be back by now." Ten minutes passed. Vidya began fidgeting. Another ten minutes, and anxiety began to creep in.

The guide ran to the back of the building and tapped on the toilet door. "Anyone inside?"

"Yes! I'm stuck! The bolt is jammed!" came Damu's muffled but unmistakable voice.

The guide called the *Dhaba* owner, and together with a staffer, they brought a crowbar. After some hard knocks and prying, the door finally gave way. Damu stepped out, embarrassed but thankful.

"Sir, you're a VIP now," the guide joked. "Bus can't start without you!"

Lakshmi and Vidya heaved a sigh of relief. Damu, dusting himself off and chuckling nervously, climbed aboard.

Just as the driver turned the ignition key, a thunderous *boom* echoed through the valley. The bus jerked to a halt. Everyone froze.

It wasn't thunder. Something was wrong.

The tourist guide's phone rang. It was the manager of the Wayanad resort. His voice was panicked. "Don't come up! A massive landslide has hit the main road to the resort. Entire sections of the road are gone. Some houses and shops were swept away. It's a disaster!"

Everyone in the bus fell silent as the guide relayed the news. A few tourists, along with the driver and guide, walked cautiously about 500 meters ahead to inspect the road.

What they saw shook them to the core.

The winding mountain road had disappeared, replaced by a mess of uprooted trees, boulders, and red mud. The ghat section was obliterated. Water still flowed through the cracks, and debris lay scattered for hundreds of meters.

One tourist muttered, "If we had left earlier..."

With his face going pale, the driver completed the sentence, "We'd have been exactly at this spot—right when it hit."

A chilling realisation dawned on everyone. The delay caused by Damu's washroom mishap had saved them all from certain death.

The entire group turned toward Damu, who stood blinking in disbelief. "I... I just got stuck. I didn't do anything heroic," he stammered.

But the crowd erupted in spontaneous applause.

"Damu, sir, that stuck bolt was our guardian angel," said a middle-aged woman.

"God has strange ways," someone added.

Even Lakshmi, though amused, couldn't help smiling. Vidya looked up proudly at her father, "Appa, you always end up saving people by accident!"

The guide called his head office in Kozhikode to explain the situation. The manager advised them to take the tourists to a nearby lodge and provide meals and shelter. He assured that alternate arrangements for return to Cochin would be made the next day.

The group was settled comfortably for the night. That evening, over dinner, tales of the "

The Man Who Delayed Death" began to circulate.

The next morning, the tourists boarded a return bus to Cochin. Unlike the tense ascent, the return journey was filled with laughter, songs, and stories. Damu, at first shy, soon joined in the chorus of a popular Hindi song.

Back in Cochin, Lakshmi called their friend Ranjith and narrated the entire episode.

There was a pause on the other end before Ranjith said with a chuckle, "Not surprised at all. I keep telling you—God has blessed Damu with a strange boon. Wherever he goes, chaos may follow, but so does salvation."

And so, the story of Damu and the landslide became yet another tale in the growing legend of the "Unintentional Saviour"—a man whose accidents often turned out to be miracles in disguise.

Damu, the Banana Peel & the Bucket of Sambar

The journey from Kedarpur to Thanjavur had begun with excitement. Damu, his wife Lakshmi, and their 12-year-old daughter Vidya were headed to attend the wedding of a cousin from Lakshmi's side. The function was to take place in a traditional marriage hall in Thanjavur, not far from the renowned **Brihadeeswarar Temple**.

Along with them travelled **Inspector Ranjith**, a close family friend of Damu's and a respected police officer. He had accepted the invitation to the wedding not only as a guest but also to take a short break from his usual routine in Kedarpur.

The family, along with Ranjith, made their way to the majestic Brihadeeswarar Temple for a divine start to the day. The sun reflected off the towering **Vimana**, casting long shadows across the temple courtyard. Vidya, full of energy, marvelled at the centuries-old carvings.

"Appa, look at this Ganesha carved so intricately!" she exclaimed.

Damu, barefoot and tiptoeing across the warm granite floor, nodded more to keep her enthusiasm alive than out of real attention. His feet longed for his slippers.

Lakshmi smiled. "Let her take in all this culture before we get to the chaos of the wedding."

Damu grumbled quietly, "Culture is hot."

Before heading to the hall, Lakshmi suggested a visit to a small, lesser-known temple near the wedding venue. The priest there had once been associated with the family.

This modest shrine held one precious relic: a **ruby-studded nose ring**, said to have been offered by a Chola queen. It was displayed in a glass case, guarded by a single security man and supervised by a middle-aged temple executive officer seated nearby.

Unbeknownst to the devotees, **three men**, dressed in traditional attire, had entered with ill intentions. Two of them approached the guard, pretending to ask about rituals, while the third slowly inched toward the case. His tool was a tiny lever hidden in his dhoti.

Just a few steps away from the sanctum where the precious ring was kept, Damu wandered, lost in thought. His musings were interrupted, no, sabotaged—by a rogue banana peel carelessly discarded on the stone floor.

In one dramatic swoop, Damu's foot slipped, and he toppled backwards, arms flailing. The third thief had just managed to pry open the case and snatched the ring when fate intervened: Damu's fall landed squarely in his path. The thief tripped over him, the nose ring flew into the air, and the thief's face kissed the ground with a resounding *thwack*, flattening his nose.

Startled devotees quickly restrained him. The temple EO, stunned, called for the police immediately.

The other two culprits disappeared into the crowd—enraged and embarrassed—and muttered revenge under their breath. One had noted the name of the man who had ruined their plan: Damu.

Later that day, the marriage hall was bustling. Garlands dangled from pillars, *Nadaswaram* notes floated through the air, and Damu was surrounded by relatives congratulating him on his "divine intervention."

The two escaped thieves had not gone far. Disguised in fresh shirts and false smiles, they entered the hall carrying empty gift boxes, easily blending in with the crowd.

Their new target: **Lakshmi's emerald-studded necklace**, which she wore with visible pride and occasional glances in every mirror.

Damu, keen to stay helpful and stay away from the press, volunteered to **serve lunch.** He carried a large bucket of **hot sambar** and served guests enthusiastically, with a mug in hand.

"The dining hall was filled with guests seated at every table, engaged in animated conversations and enjoying their meals. Among them, Lakshmi and Vidya sat at a table tucked away at the far end of the hall, close to the kitchen, where the clatter of utensils and the aroma of freshly prepared food drifted into the room." They chatted, unaware of the two thieves slowly creeping behind them.

One thief pretended to talk loudly on a mobile phone, repeatedly using "Vidya" in conversation —he had heard them talking earlier. The other thief, with a **small cutter hidden in his palm**, crept up behind Lakshmi, hoping the distraction would buy enough time.

"At that moment, Damu rounded the corner, a bucket swinging in his hand, and headed toward the table where Lakshmi and Vidya sat. In an instant, a sharp glint caught his eye — the cutter. "Without hesitation, he **hurled a full mug of steaming sambar** directly into the thief's face.

"Ayyyo!" the thief screamed, clutching his eyes and nose. In panic, he turned and ran—only to knock into a pillar, smearing himself in tamarind gravy.

The second thief turned to run—but **Ranjith**, already suspicious of their behaviour throughout the event, blocked his path with a swift move.

Ranjith caught him by the collar and looked towards the stunned crowd. "Don't worry. These two won't touch anyone's jewellery again."

The local **wrestler**, present as a guest, helped Ranjith restrain them both until the police arrived. Ranjith flashed his ID. "Inspector Ranjith, Kedarpur Police. These men are temple thieves on the run."

The Guests had paused their meal, but now the hall erupted in laughter and cheers. The **caterer** shouted, "From today, this will be called *Hero Sambar*!"

Lakshmi wiped the remnants of the sambar from her necklace and said, "Next time, I'll just wear a garland instead!"

Vidya giggled. "Appa saved us again! First the temple, now with sambar!"

Ranjith shook his head in admiration. "Damu, you're a one-man anti-crime squad. We'll make you an honorary constable."

Damu, bashfully, replied, "I was only trying to serve lunch. It's not my fault that criminals keep running into me."

As the evening cooled, the family rode back to their hotel, exhausted but happy. Social media buzzed with a short reel—Vidya had posted: *"Appa, Protector of Temples & Sambar!"*

Ranjith, seated beside Damu, smiled and said, "You know, in another life, you'd have made a very unique police officer."

Damu laughed. "I think I'll stick to my desk and my paperweight."

Lakshmi added lovingly, "And maybe next time, wear shoes with some grip."

The auto passed a small shop. Outside, a boy tossed a banana peel into the street.

Vidya and Damu locked eyes and said in unison, "Oh! No! Not again!"

"Train to Trouble — *Pickles & Parcels*"

It began, as most of Damu's misadventures did, with a perfectly innocent phone call and an overly enthusiastic, "Yes, of course, Subbu!"

"Anna," crooned cousin Subbu from Chennai, "I've sent you my special tender mango pickles. The tin is packed safely in a cardboard box. There's a big letter 'D' on the lid — you'll spot it faster than a crow finds pongal."

Damu imagined spoonfuls of salty, tangy heaven melting over hot rice and agreed without once checking if the stars were aligned to warn him of yet another impending fiasco.

The next morning, he zigzagged through Kedarpur Railway Station and located the parcel delivery counter. The overworked clerk glanced at his ID, ticked off a column, and waved vaguely toward a stack of boxes.

Damu's eyes fell on one with a giant, hand-painted "D." Perfect. He hoisted it triumphantly, thanked every nearby human in sight, and waddled off to the scooter stand.

Just minutes later, Syed and Prakash — loyal (but not particularly bright) henchmen of smuggler Vikram — collected another box, also marked with a bold "D." They raced it back to their boss.

Vikram sliced it open with flair... only to find a lone tin labelled *Subbu's Super Spicy Tender Mangoes.*

There was a moment of stunned silence. Then came the twitch. Then the volcanic roar.

"Three crores worth of diamonds — Gone! And you bring me achar?!"

He grabbed the box and read the return address aloud: "Damodar, Kedarpur."

"Get the car!" he bellowed.

The gang sped off, the air thick with panic, chilli-scented pickle, and bad decisions.

Back at home, Damu ceremoniously opened *his* parcel, ready to dive into pickle paradise. Instead, out slid a small black velvet pouch.

"Subbu's pickles now come in designer handbags?" he muttered.

He untied the pouch and six glittering stones rolled out, winking like traffic lights on a rainy night.

He blinked. "Lakshmi, do pickles sparkle now?"

Lakshmi took one look and gasped. "These aren't pickles... these are you know those... expensive things!"

"Pebbles?" Damu offered.

"Diamonds, Damu! DIA-MONDS!"

The room spun with panic. Lakshmi, ever the grounded one, picked up the phone and called Inspector Ranjith — family friend, top cop, and veteran witness to Damu-induced chaos.

Ranjith arrived in record time, his eyes scanning the living room like a barcode reader. One look at the stones and he gave a low whistle.

"Subbu's new venture into luxury condiments?"

"Very funny," Lakshmi muttered. "Check the address. Damu probably picked up the wrong box — saw 'D' and assumed it stood for *dinner delight*."

Ranjith flipped the box flap. The sender's address was blank.

"Fake," he said. "Which means the rightful owners are probably on their way — and they won't be looking for pickle tastings."

Meanwhile, Vikram's sedan screeched to a halt a few streets away. He spotted a police jeep parked at Damu's gate. His face twitched again.

"Perfect. Cops already sniffing around," he muttered, tossing Syed and Prakash out of the car. "Stakeout. Watch the house. And no more screw-ups."

Back inside, Ranjith phoned his deputy Vinay Kumar. "Plainclothes. Position near Damu's house. Two suspicious men should be easy to spot — probably dressed like bushes."

Vinay soon spotted Syed and Prakash lurking behind a lamppost pretending to be casual. He updated Ranjith, who by now was sipping Damu's filter coffee while planning his next move.

"I'll keep the diamonds at the station tonight," said Ranjith. "They won't risk breaking in if the house is empty."

The next morning, Lakshmi picked up her jute bag. "I'll be back in ten minutes. Just getting vegetables."

Syed and Prakash perked up and texted Vikram: *Target leaving the house.*

Vinay trailed behind Lakshmi from a safe distance, relaying her every step.

Vikram, now twice as furious and half as patient, arrived in a battered sedan. "Plan B: kidnap and ransom," he growled.

He parked up ahead. Syed and Prakash got into position. One pretended to admire bananas while the other prepared a handkerchief soaked in chloroform.

"Boss," Vinay crackled through the comms, "they're moving in."

Ranjith's jeep rolled forward like a silent predator on wheels.

Lakshmi, engrossed in tomatoes, never saw Syed approach. One hand clamped her mouth; the other dragged her backwards. Prakash flung open the sedan door.

But Lakshmi wasn't easy bait. Her elbow found Prakash's ribs. He yelped but managed to shove her inside.

The car roared to life — and screeched to a halt as Ranjith's jeep blocked the road.

Tomatoes rolled. Vendors scattered. Chaos ensued.

Ranjith leapt out, gun drawn. "Police! Hands up!"

Vikram reached for his revolver — but froze as Ranjith's gun tapped on his window like a polite but firm request.

Syed and Prakash tried to flee, but Vinay tackled them with professional flair. Lakshmi, dazed but safe, was sent home in the jeep.

At the station, Vikram sulked as the diamonds were presented on the table.

"Three crores," Ranjith said. "And now a few crores worth of jail time."

Later, the *real* pickle parcel was returned to Damu, who received it like it were a national treasure.

Lakshmi pried it open and smiled. "Seems like Subbu finally got it right."

Vidya walked in just in time to steal the first spoonful. "Mmm! Worth all the drama."

Subbu called that evening, sheepish. "Anna, I wrote 'D' for 'Damu'. Who knew diamonds would also come looking for the same letter?"

"Next time," Damu said, "just send me the recipe."

A week later, Damu received a commendation from the Railway Police for his *inadvertent role* in cracking a diamond smuggling case. It came in a box tied with a ribbon shaped, annoyingly, like a giant letter D.

Damu tossed the ribbon but kept the certificate — proudly sticking a note on the fridge:

"NO PARCELS ACCEPTED UNLESS THEY LEAK OIL AND SMELL OF MANGOES."

Somewhere in jail, Vikram sneezed at the memory of pickle brine. Ranjith polished his badge. And Damu? He enjoyed a plate of curd rice with mango pickle, but was sceptical about every cardboard box that dared to display the letter D.

Damu and the Resort of Restless Relics

The plan sounded foolproof when Inspector Pratap first suggested it.

"Anna," he said to his elder brother Ranjith, "The Bengaluru Traffic will drive Damu Uncle and family mad".

"I've booked them a quiet resort on the outskirts. Three days of birdsong, then straight to my wedding."

"Brilliant," Ranjith agreed, confident that nothing in the universe could sabotage so simple a scheme—clearly forgetting the cosmic magnet that was Damodar.

The battered taxi coughed up red dust as it stopped before Silent Trails Resort. Bougainvillaea twined around wrought iron gates, and a signboard promised "Nature, Nurture, and NO Network."

The regular receptionist had reported sick. In her place stood a nervy part-timer named Kishore who flipped through the ledger, saw the surname "Damodar," and absent-mindedly allocated Suite 21—the owner's strictly private, "only with permission" cottage. Kishore did not know this; Kishore merely liked the handwriting in Box 21.

Lakshmi admired the antique teak furniture. Vidya sat down on the bed, exclaiming, "They've even got a rosewood wardrobe!" Damu eyed the silence beyond the windows and thought, "No honking, no boss, no pollution. Heaven."

"Lakshmi, we have an electric kettle here with instant coffee sachets. Give me a cup of coffee," said Damu.

Heaven curdled by 11 p.m. Strange thuds echoed behind the walls, metal clanged somewhere below, and once, a clear *ting ting ting* tapped Morse-like before retreating.

"Wind," Damu mumbled, rolling over.

"No wind makes mechanical noises," Lakshmi hissed, clutching her pillow.

Vidya sat up, phone flashlight on. "Appa, the wardrobe just rattled."

They slept in fits, counting noises instead of sheep. At dawn, a bleary Damu shuffled to reception, but Kishore had vanished, replaced by a gardener who claimed ignorance and fled to prune hibiscus.

One of the bulbs in the room flickered. Damu usually carried a small kit containing a screwdriver, flashlight, small screws and nails, and a tiny hammer.

Determined to stop a flickering bulb, Damu unscrewed the switchboard cover after breakfast. One loose wire poked out like a stubborn nose hair. He pushed it back—*click!*

A low rumble answered. The rosewood wardrobe shuddered, slid sideways, and revealed a dim stairwell corkscrewing into the earth.

Lakshmi gasped. Vidya's eyes foresaw an exciting adventure. Damu rubbed his chin. "Either this is the spa or the secret pantry."

Flashlights in hand, they descended. The tunnel meandered—good solid granite giving way to rough bricks until, maybe 500 metres later, it opened into a cavernous storeroom lit by a single industrial bulb.

Stacked on wooden pallets were ancient bronze idols—Ganeshas, Natarajas, celestial attendants—wrapped in bubble packs and export crates labelled "Ayurvedic Grinding Stones – Handle with Care."

"I now know, there must be another opening to the godown from outside, where the loading operations are carried out," Vidya said.

They carefully explored the godown and found a hidden door locked from the outside.

Back at reception, resort owner Mr. Ravi Shetty returned from a business trip, discovered Suite 21 occupied, and nearly choked on his sunflower seeds.

"That cottage?" he barked. "Who authorised it?"

When Kishore admitted his ledger blunder, Shetty's panic sharpened into malice. He marched to the cottage, bolted the outer door, and activated portable signal jammers the size of lunchboxes.

Meanwhile, at the godown, Vidya whispered, "Temple theft ring." Damu reached for his phone and said, "I will inform Ranjith." He tried to dial Ranjith's number—no response. He peered into the mobile and said, "No signal."

They walked back up the stairs into the suite.

Vidya checked her mobile and found no bars. "Zero. They've blocked us."

Footsteps retreated outside. Damu tried to open the front door. "It's locked from the outside."

"We are trapped."

How to send the message to Ranjith?

Vidya remembered a shallow attic she'd spotted through a ceiling vent at the godown where the idols were stacked. She quickly ran down the steps toward the godown. Grabbing a rickety wooden ladder, she clambered up, shimmied across dusty beams, and found a loose clay tile. Beneath it, a hand-sized gap breathed in fresh air... and one backpack-strength mobile signal. She typed furiously:

Vidya ➜ Ranjith Uncle

Locked in Suite 21, Silent Trails Resort. Smuggling idols. Owner hostile. SOS.

One tick. Two ticks. Blue ticks!

Ranjith's reply came quickly: *On my way with Pratap. Tell Appa not to touch anything explosive.*

Vidya slid back down. "Rescue inbound."

Less than forty minutes later, two unmarked SUVs rolled through the gate. Inspector Ranjith hopped out, followed by a groom-to-be in track pants—Pratap—whose wedding sherwani was presumably safer in a closet.

They bypassed reception and entered the owner's cabin and handcuffed a protesting Shetty.

They ordered the receptionist to retrieve the Suite 21 keys from Shetty's cabin and unlock Suite 21.

"Everybody okay?" Pratap asked.

Lakshmi nodded; Damu held up a cup filled with half-drunk coffee prepared with the electric kettle and instant coffee powder.

Ranjith led a team down the secret stairs, filming rows of idols. Shetty, dragged along, muttered excuses about "ancestral collection," which dissolved when Ranjith pointed to *Made in Pakistan* export stickers.

Syed and Basheer—the noise-making labourers—were found hiding behind crates; they surrendered after Pratap threatened to postpone his honeymoon to handle interrogation personally.

Damu's family entered. Rumours had spread:

"Two days later, at a grand Bengaluru marriage hall decked with orchids, a roar went up when Damu Uncle uncovered an international idol racket!"

"Vidya hacked through bricks to send GPS!"

"Lakshmi faced gunmen with rolling pins!" (That last embellishment came courtesy of gossiping aunties.)

Pratap, now in pristine sherwani, greeted them. "Thanks to you three, my guest list includes half the Crime Branch—and we're starting exactly on time."

During dinner, a guest asked Damu how he discovered the idols. He shrugged, spooning ***Payasam***. "Loose wiring. Always fix what flickers."

Vidya rolled her eyes. "Appa, maybe become an electrician full-time. World crime rates will plummet."

Lakshmi smiled, adjusting her silk pallu. "At least we got three nights' free stay. Breakfast could've been better, though."

The resort was seized by authorities; Suite 21 is now sealed behind yellow tape. A new signboard appeared outside:

NOTICE: This property is under investigation.

For quiet vacations, kindly choose any place where Damu is not visiting.

Back in Kedarpur, Damu taped two Post-its on the fridge:

1. "Switchboards first, sightseeing later."
2. "Ask the resort for Wi-Fi strength before paying the deposit."

The second note fluttered loose that evening and, with typical timing, landed over the light switch. Damu reached to straighten it, and Lakshmi yelled, "Stop! Check for wardrobes!"

He froze mid-stretch, then laughed. "From now on, I carry along with my toolbox... and maybe a spare idol detector."

Vidya raised her phone. "Say cheese, Ghostbuster."

The click captured a family still wide-eyed from adventure, yet certain that the next trip—whatever the universe sent them-would contain the usual dose of Damu-style mischief, hidden doors, and enough humour to keep even haunted resorts from feeling scary.

"Damu's Hyderabad Hustle"

Damu's latest misadventure began the moment his boss dangled a plum assignment in front of him.

"Hyderabad needs your magic touch," the man said, wiping chutney from his moustache. "Sign the vendor contract, audit the books, charm them with your... er... Damodarness."

Damu heard only two words: ***Hyderabad trip***. It was the perfect excuse to pacify Lakshmi's elder brother, Anand, Vice President at a swanky software firm and relentless cheerleader of the city.

"You people never visit!" Anand lamented on every family call. "Our biryani alone is worth the airfare. There's Charminar, Tank Bund, Ramoji Film City—Hyderabad is history stuffed inside a tech wrapper!"

When Damodar announced the trip at dinner, Lakshmi clapped, and Vidya whooped.

The train rolled into Secunderabad at sunrise. Anand arrived in a gleaming company CAB—air-conditioned, lemon-scented, and boasting a dashboard deity that changed colours.

"First rule," Anand said, driving through necklace-shaped Tank Bund, "eat breakfast before traffic eats us."

His apartment in Himayatnagar overlooked a park of power-walking uncles. Lakshmi settled into family gossip, Vidya raided Anand's bookshelf of tech comics, and Damu donned a blazer to conquer the vendor meeting in Begumpet.

During the meeting, Damu realised that he had lost his phone. He checked his pockets. No phone. Cold sweat blossomed. He tried to recollect where he could have misplaced it. The last hour of the meeting was an introduction and briefing, which required no use of the mobile. Just before the morning tea break, he realised the necessity of the mobile, as some files had to be referred to. Just as Damu was pondering what to do, the peon came to him and said someone had come to meet him and was waiting at the reception. Damu walked towards the entrance and found the driver smiling at him. The driver, a mild-mannered man with earnest eyes, said, "Sir! You left this in my cab this morning—from Himayatnagar to Begumpet?"

Relief flooded Damu. "Ayyo! You're a lifesaver." Grateful beyond measure, he blurted, while receiving the mobile from him, "Can you take my family for Balaji Darshan at Birla Balaji Mandir?"

The driver said, "Sure, sir."

"What is your name?" Damu asked.

"My name's Ravi, sir."

"Ok, Ravi, come to Himayatnagar, where you picked me up today."

Ravi nodded and left.

The next morning, Ravi arrived with a freshly washed sedan, windows gleaming, engine purring like a cat that drank all the cream. Vidya hopped in front, notebook ready.

"Show me Hyderabad like I'm a YouTuber," she declared.

Ravi, warming up, became a fountain of trivia.

Charminar? Built by Mohammed Quli Qutb Shah in 1591.

Falaknuma? Palace of mirrors and a dining table for 101 guests.

Hussain Sagar? Buddha statue weighs 350 tons.

Vidya scribbled, awestruck. Damu nodded like a tourist absorbing cultural calories. Lakshmi, from the back seat, enjoyed the breeze and Ravi's gentle commentary.

Yet every few kilometres, Ravi's phone pinged. Each message drained colour from his face. Vidya noticed the tremor in his hands. Something was wrong.

At Birla Balaji Mandir, the marble idol glittered under the morning light. Ravi parked and offered to wait by the cab. After the darshan, Damu, Lakshmi, and Vidya got into the cab. Damu told him to proceed towards Hotel Kamath. He asked Ravi to join them for lunch.

Hotel Kamath is a vegetarian landmark where dosas arrive wider than steering wheels. Anand joined them straight from the office, ID card swinging.

As plates of thali arrived, Vidya whispered to Anand about Ravi's twitchy demeanour. Anand quietly observed their guest: sweat on the brow despite the AC, eyes flicking to the entrance.

Halfway through badam halwa, Ravi excused himself to take a call. Vidya followed at a discreet distance and overheard:

"Sir, I'll deliver the box at Chaderghat by three. Please... my sister is alone."

She returned wide-eyed. Anand's tech-savvy brain clicked into gear.

"Ravi," Anand began gently when the driver returned, "Is someone forcing you to move something illegal?"

Ravi's fork froze. Tears brimmed. The whole story spilt: a gang had seized his sister's nursing college documents back in Warangal and threatened worse if he didn't transport small tech packages hidden in his cab. Today's drop was critical. Damu's jaw dropped—he'd invited extortion to lunch!

Anand excused himself and dialled a Warangal DCP he'd befriended during a corporate CSR project. Within minutes, local police were dispatched to secure Ravi's sister's hostel.

Next, Anand called his college friend Shilpa, now an ACP in Hyderabad Traffic. "Need an RTO-level sting on a cab suspected of tech smuggling. Location: Chaderghat. Meet us near Musi Bridge."

Shilpa, always game for Friday excitement, assembled the units.

Ravi drove, heart pounding, Damu beside him like a bewildered bodyguard, Lakshmi and Vidya behind, and Anand tailing in his car.

Near the Chaderghat warehousing lanes, two men flagged the cab. One wore aviators, the other sported a scar. Ravi parked. Scarface tapped the boot.

Before the boot could pop, sirens wailed. RTO jeeps boxed them in. ACP Shilpa strode over, Anand in tow.

"Show me your boot," she ordered.

Scarface tried to run; Damu, stepping out clumsily, accidentally extended a foot. The man tripped into a puddle of chilli-coloured water from a nearby pani puri cart. Aviator raised his hands as officers cuffed him.

Inside the boot: dozens of smartphones, microchips, and RFID readers—hot property en route to a counterfeit factory.

Shilpa nodded at Anand. "Thanks for the tip. Who's the kingpin?"

Ravi stammered a name: Raghu "King"—a local transport contractor controlling half the shady couriers in Old City.

Anand grinned. "Raghu King supplies to our office canteen. I can lure him with a fake order for five industrial refrigerators."

Shilpa's eyes sparkled. "Done. Operation Icebox begins tonight."

That evening, Raghu fell like a sack of idli batter at his warehouse when Shilpa's team stormed the place. Anand, wearing a visitor badge, pointed at a stack of fridges. Inside were more stolen gadgets.

Raghu protested—until Shilpa showed live CCTV of Warangal police escorting Ravi's sister to safety.

Two days later, Ravi's sister phoned to thank the entire Damodar clan. Ravi, now free of blackmail, arrived with a new SIM card and a relieved smile.

At Paradise Biryani, they celebrated. Lakshmi insisted on double dessert. Vidya recorded a vlog titled *How to Bust a Smuggling Ring with One Family Trip.*

Damu raised a spoon of double ka meetha. "All I wanted was a peaceful assignment and some time with family."

Anand laughed. "Next project, bhava, we schedule you in business class flights only—no more cabs."

Vidya rolled her eyes. "Appa could foil crime even in an elevator."

Damu toasted them with Hyderabad's finest Irani chai. "Trouble follows me like coriander on everything. At least the chai is authentic."

Across the table, Ravi grinned. "Sir, if you ever visit Hyderabad again, please call me."

Damu blurted out, "But maybe we stick to temple visits—no hidden cargo."

Outside, the city lights flickered along the Musi, oblivious to the fact that, once again, Damu's accidental heroics had untangled crime and woven one more hilarious story into the tapestry of Hyderabad's night.

****

Vocabulary

Haveli:	A big, old-style Indian house
Enclosure:	A closed area for animals in a zoo
Sauntered:	walked slowly and calmly
Bugler:	A person who blows a small trumpet
Clattered:	Made a loud, rattling noise
Oblivious:	Not knowing what's happening
Torrential:	Very heavy and fast (like rain)
Culvert:	A pipe or drain under a road for water to flow
Debris:	Broken pieces and trash
Toppled:	Fell over suddenly
Thudding:	Making a heavy, dull sound
Glint:	A quick flash of light
Artefact:	An old or special object made by people
Smuggler:	Someone who secretly moves illegal things
Replica:	A copy of something real
Kidnapped:	Taken away by someone without permission
Commendation:	A formal praise or award
Thwack:	A loud hit or slap sound
Muffled:	Not clear or loud (like through a wall)
Signal jammers:	Devices that block mobile signals

DISCLAIMER

This is a work of fiction. Names, characters, places, events, and incidents are either the product of the author's imagination or used in a fictitious manner. Any resemblance to actual persons, living or dead, or to actual events or locales is purely coincidental.

While the stories in *Legend of Damu – Part 2* may draw inspiration from everyday life, they are intended purely for entertainment. The character of Damodar, though delightfully entangled in heroic misadventures, is fictional and not based on any real individual.

The author and publisher do not endorse or encourage any risky, unlawful, or comically misguided behaviour depicted in these stories. Readers are advised to enjoy the content with a sense of humour and an appreciation for harmless chaos.

EPILOGUE

In "Legend of Damu - Part 2," follow Damu and his family through eight captivating episodes filled with humour, warmth, and unexpected heroism as they navigate everything from temple escapades to tech-smuggling misadventures. As Damu, along with his determined wife Lakshmi and astute daughter Vidya, unwittingly unravels a smuggling ring in Hyderabad, their ordinary lives transform into extraordinary tales of chaos and courage. These stories celebrate the magic of life's small moments, reminding us that even the most unassuming individuals can become heroes through their gentle spirits and unwavering love.

ABOUT THE AUTHOR

R. Kalyana Krishnan (fondly called Kalyan) is a gifted storyteller who finds extraordinary inspiration in the ordinary moments of life. With a deep appreciation for humour, warmth, and human quirks, he brings to life the character of Damodar, a simple man who unintentionally becomes a hero in the most unexpected situations.

Kalyan's writing combines heart, wit, and gentle life lessons, making his stories especially appealing to children, parents, and grandparents alike. His tales are rooted in Indian family values and filled with relatable characters, gentle suspense, and a generous dose of laughter.

Through Damodar's accidental adventures and unplanned acts of courage, the author reminds readers that heroism doesn't always wear a cape—it often wears a raincoat, carries a flask, or fumbles its way into doing the right thing.

Kalyan draws inspiration from his surroundings and his own life experiences. His grandchildren —Aryan, Shlok, and Ishika—play a special role in shaping his stories. Their curiosity, energy, and joy often spark the next twist in Damu's unpredictable journey.

Legend of Damu - Part 2 is not just a continuation of a tale, but a celebration of everyday courage, family bonds, and the belief that even the most unlikely among us can be heroes.